Blurbs

Rachel Jeffries

Lizard Ventures

Lone Tree, Colorado

Scottsdale, Arizona

To Katie,

who received many of these in the
middle of the night and told me
they were beautiful.

These blurbs will never be as
beautiful as your friendship has
been to me.

xoxo

Contents

Blurbs

This is a book of paragraphs.

Of thoughts. Of streams of consciousness.

Of love. Of loneliness.

This is a book about every person's search to find what it is that makes them feel invincible, and every person's struggle to win that internal war which rages within them.

Do not read this all at once. Read it a paragraph at a time.

This book is not a shot of tequila.

It is a cup of tea on a cold, winter afternoon in Colorado. Sip it.

Blurbs

Ear Aches

"Because I'm listening" — they
were relatively inconsequential words,

but when put together

they sounded

like the most lovely thing in the
world

and I wondered again

whether I had been wrong

to write him off so soon.

Blurred Lines

The anticipation is the most bittersweet kind of despair. It is what keeps you going and makes you stop. It is a standstill and it is awful and wonderful all at the same time until one day your friend asks have you heard and no you haven't and you don't want to but she tells you anyway and suddenly there is nothing sweet about the anticipation anymore.

It

is

gone.

A third party that is gory and miserable barges in on your idle state and you wake up in the morning wanting nothing more than to go back to bed and the time when the lines were invitingly blurry and not so brutally clear.

<u>Consistency</u>

Every once in a while I return to that funny state of mind where I catch myself wondering

if ...

      maybe this time ...

          you'll be different.

But of course, that time never comes -- not at least until even more time has passed and like clockwork

I

have

fallen

back into my foolish pattern

of hopelessly loving you,

and hopelessly loving the way you

never

cease

to disappoint me.

Stage Fright

I was almost going to ask what you
were doing on Saturday and might
you want to do something with me,
but my constant fear that you
would reject me even more
obviously than you already had
kept me from asking you what I was
dying to know and kept me from
preventing all these *what ifs* that
now consume my heart.

Absence

What I miss most is the way you smiled at me, like I mattered to you. Not in a romantic way, just in general. I miss seeing you and knowing you were my friend and knowing there was the possibility you might even be something more.

But,

I don't see you anymore and even your memory no longer loves me

and the only thing that greets me in the morning is my own despair in the mirror.

Mute

The words never come to me like
I want them to. They laugh and
betray me when I need them most.

Those foul, fickle things.

They toy with my mind like you
toy with my heart. If words were
my friends, then I wouldn't be
standing

p a r a l y z e d

in a fog
of my own
brokenness.

I wouldn't be ruthlessly haunted by my most wonderful memories as if they were terrible ghosts. If words really loved me, then you would know how much I really love you.

<u>Euphoria</u>

My heart smiled at you and you
winked back at me and suddenly I
was drowning again in that
delightfully treacherous hope you
would never let me go.

Fogged In

The loneliness is a dense and
endless fog that muffles the song
of your laugh under a blanket of
gray

and

I wonder

if maybe

I can't do anything else

       but just stay

              lost

in this miserable weather.

Directions

It is embarrassing how much I think about you and it is funny how I am too scared to throw away my gilded compass and just lose myself in my dreams.

The Thief

The climax – that is what everyone should avoid. Because, after the climax – after that singular splendid moment – everything else is a disappointment.

The climax is a thief in the night.

It sneaks by when you are asleep. You wake up when the sky turns sad with the garish light of the sun. It occurs to you that the cool evening stars have fled and you spend your life dying,

dying altogether too quickly,

while you wait for something even more magical to sparkle in your eyes, for some event to tie a blue bow around all your prettiest dreams.

But, those dreams are lies and that beautiful blue bow is soiled by the dirt of reality.

The climax was glorious, but never as glorious as you hoped it would be and so you are left to waste your days - blinded - always

14

dreaming of something bigger and being disappointed when that something never comes. You can see nothing but that which you imagine and hope to soon be true. The more days you spend painting an imaginary picture of that perfect climax, the less enchanting your memory of the actual climax becomes - its golden quality tarnishes as it sits under the rain which pours down ceaselessly from the storm clouds in your heart.

You are left penniless,

the rain

having washed all your glittery
things away.

You stand

                alone

in an empty room

with nothing but the sharp shards
of your false hopes lying
shattered underneath your bloody,
unfeeling feet.

<u>S</u>

It will only be beautiful until
the ending when that final period
will

push

my

heart

off

a

cliff

and I will close the book and it
will be like falling just an
unbearably long way down as I

wonder why the story was even
started at all.

The Muddled Mind

I try to write. Supposedly, writing things down is helpful when you want to clear your mind. I can't though. I'll never be able to clear my mind of you because you are stashed away like spare change in every dusty corner of my imagination.

Up and Away

You tell yourself not to get your
hopes up. You hang on to reality
as the colorful balloons filled
with lovely thoughts try to float
you away. You think you're safe
this close to the ground. You
think it won't hurt when you fall
because the balloons have barely
lifted you, but you're wrong.

The

fall

still bruises your knees

and those purple, yellow smudges
won't fade

until your heart forgets,

which it almost never does.

Pin Cushions

After   a   while,   the   heartache
becomes comfortable and familiar.

It gets easier

to keep on with the devil you know

than allow yourself

to fall in love

with the angel you don't.

It is only when your friend says
that he probably just keeps you on
the hook, that he probably just
uses you as a confidence boost
because he knows you'll always be

there, and that you really do not want to be that girl whose desperate heart is so easily within his reach...it is only then you realize how stupid you've been, safeguarding your heartache like it's grandmother's pearls, and wearing your sunglasses to avoid the glare of reality which always demands to be seen.

It's awful.

It is awful because you knew it the whole time, but you were able to cushion the truth just enough that it couldn't shatter your

fragile hopes with its mean, sharp
edges.

Green Lights

I find myself falling in love with
you again, morning after morning,
as I drive to school.

One Day

I wait in anticipation for the words

that never come

and the smiles

that I never catch.

The Director

In the movies, love stories are
easier.

Even the on-screen love stories
filled with drama

and mixed signals

and questions of who-slept-with-
who are easier

than this boring reality

of you and me.

Screenwriters make obvious what
each character means to say and
directors show those moments
where it is clear what each

character really feels. To the
viewers, there's no question
that she loves him and that he
really is sorry. But,

in real life,

even the real feelings you have

are things

I can only guess at

and even the words you've said
to me

are puzzle pieces

I can't seem to fit.

Infections

The jealousy is a sharp edge on a
dirty piece of paper that makes
your fingers look ugly and your
blood disgusting.

Infidelity

The words do not like each other so they refuse to make sentences.

The sentence cheated on the other so they have no common ground on which to build a paragraph.

The paragraphs have lost their money and can't afford to buy enough for a good story.

The story is never written because the words

won't

allow it.

Burn Out

I am paralyzed by the steel grip
of exhaustion that

f r e e z e s

all the smiles that try to warm my
icy heart.

The Yellow Car

His smile has the awful effect of
lessening my capacity for wonder
because

in that charming moment

my eyes are fooled into believing

nothing else

might be so exciting.

Self - destruction

Insecurity is a parasite.

It burns

everything inside you,

but only you can feel the smoke

as it blackens your lungs

and poisons your mind.

Love turns to jealously and happiness turns to hollowness. The parasite strips you. It leaves you sickly and falling – falling down,

down,

down into nothing.

Exhaustion

It gets hard acting like it isn't hard. Every morning you wake up early to paint your smile on your face and tell yourself

that you're okay,

that you're not jealous,

that you're totally fine

being the girl with the beautiful best friend who everyone else is in love with.

Dehydration

My frozen heart is

heavy

with the weight of the thousand
tears I haven't cried.

Grandfather Clock

How time flies and hurts my heart.

Empty Parking Lots

I am in love with this idea, this
rose-colored fantasy of being in
love. It is when the credits have
finished rolling and I am outside
the theater,

walking

into

the

night

which is so silent and beautiful
that no one dares to speak and
bring the infinite possibilities

that sparkle within the stars back
to reality.

It is better to be quiet.

It is better to be whispered to by
the night than by another because
only the moon knows what the heart
is desperate to hear.

<u>Cravings</u>

The distant sirens and the
chirping crickets are not so
annoying when heard through the
bedroom window in the still shadow
of midnight, when the heart is
heavy and the mind is weak. They
are not so annoying when the heart
craves company and the mind craves
distraction. The sirens soothe the
heart because

all it yearns for is rescue,

the crickets numb the mind because

all it needs is p e a c e.

<u>Midnight</u>

The goodbye comes sooner than
expected, what once was welcomed
as a cool rain to wash away the
past is a terrible thunderstorm.

It

beats

down

on your shoulders and suddenly you
can't tell whether the water

dripping

down

your face is God's rain or your
own stupid tears.
The clock ticks.

You can hear it even through the deafening rain. No matter how much time you have, it is never enough. When the zeroes line up and the clock strikes twelve, you'll still be rushing down that staircase.

You'll never be ready to go.

You'll always be too close.

The goodbye can't be avoided.

You can't

turn back

the clock,

even when both of your lips are close and the only thing in the world you want to be able to do is pause in time and kiss the

impossible   kiss   that   is   finally
possible at last.

Evening Tea

The water boils. It screams, demanding to be heard and tended to. It is an unavoidable distraction.

Lipstick

One day the sun will shine a
little brighter and the sky will
seem a little bluer and the girl
in the striped dress will refuse
to touch up her smudged lips
because

then

the sweetness

will only be

a memory.

Addiction

Flattery is the sweetest poison. It's addicting. The minute you taste it, you only want more, but no matter how much you drink it is never as exhilarating as that first high.

After a while, the memory is more than a memory. It is a divine vision that is made all the more delightful and fuzzy by an impossible golden filter.

August

He smiled at me from the track
like I was the only girl he wanted
to see.

And, it was raining.

The rain makes everything sweeter.

Despair

Another summer, another year, day after day after day as the books pile up and the phone stays silent and you don't even understand how it is that you've come to feel so lost and how it is that you'll get through today, tomorrow, or the next thirty years.

Overripe

I am worried that I am too serious
and that I'll be thirty years old
before I've even blinked and,

all of a sudden,

I'll really have to be mature and
adult-like before I've even had a
chance to act young and dumb.

What if I waste my youth?

That is my biggest fear

because

it is something I really think I
might do.

Bad Habits

I like that he hurts me without even knowing it. There is something unconventionally romantic about our relationship. `

The way that we retreat back into the familiarity of our teasing. The way we make plans

and break them

and never figure things out.

<u>Timeline</u>

We have two weeks left.

Less than two weeks really.

Ten days actually.

Ten days for what there could have been

                            two years.

And, who knows if we'll figure something out

but why

does the clock have to tick so loudly?

It makes it impossible to dream.

False Advertisement

Hate is like a poisoned perfume which disguises its toxic qualities in a pretty, silver bottle.

Your vanity tricks you.

You love the pretty perfume.

You spray it every morning and every day and every night.

Its subtle layers eventually become an overwhelming stench. It dampens your senses and seeps into your skin, poisons your blood and your brain.

Until,

one morning,

you spray

the

very

last

drop

from the pretty bottle and

you realize

as you fall dead

to the floor

what was inside it

all along.

The Allusion

Life can easily trick you. It is easy to become blind by this notion that you know everything, that you understand all of the world's subtleties, the mind's games, and the heart's misconceptions. You get high on the ultimate drug, which is pride. Pride in this almost religious belief that you, and only you, really understand, that only you really can grasp what it is to be alive, what it is to be weak.

There is a sick irony that I have come to recognize. It is in the alley ways of my inadequacy that I am my most reckless. Inadequacy is the dealer who lurks in shadows, just visible enough that you can see him but hidden enough that you cannot see the gun tucked in his belt.

You think because you see him you are safe.

You think because you are not scared of the shadows that you are brave.

Awareness of self is a double-edged sword.

It is that which helps you find the dealer, but it is also that which gets you shot.

Traces

There's a difference between loving him and being *in love* with him. This difference is crucial. It is ultimately that straw which has the power to

b r e a k

the camel's back

or make him

stronger.

In high school, it is easy *to love* someone. It is easy to fall for those qualities which make a person desirable. It is not easy to be *in love* with someone because it is when you're *in love* with someone that the lines begin to blur. Being *in love* is a bittersweet despair. That which makes it unbearable is also what makes it addicting. It is a drug which is impossible to quit. It stays in your bloodstream. Even when the days have turned into years

you'll

never

be

completely

clean.

<u>Punctuation</u>

Space is more than the final frontier. It's the pauses. It is the split second moments that last a life time.

Produce

There are three kinds of people:

the cool, the marginally-less-cool-
but-still-socially-acceptable,

and the awkward.

"The awkward" doesn't just apply
to obviously awkward people,
meaning those people who just
inherently lack social skills.
"The awkward" is a classification,
like race or sex. You can't avoid
it. It just is.

Whether you fall in this category depends on whether you are a peach or an orange.

A peach has a thin skin and a rich, juicy inside. When you eat a peach, it's easy to get to the good stuff. An orange has a thick peel. You have to work to eat an orange. You have to really want it. An orange isn't like a peach. You can't just grab it off the kitchen counter and bite in.

You have to peel the orange,
bit

by

bit

by

bit,

until finally you get to the fruity part...but, even then, the work is not finished because you still have to break the little segmented orange pieces apart to eat.

Wouldn't it have been easier to just eat the peach? And, isn't the peach a more worthwhile nutritious endeavor? It is better than an orange, juicier; an orange is watery and sometimes too tart or covered with that annoying white pulp-y stuff. The orange will never be as easy or as satisfying as the peach.

The oranges will stay left out, accumulating dust on the counter top. They will be

tossed aside

by everyone, except for "the awkward" because oranges are all they have to eat when the peaches are gone.

Shiftable

You have got to make your own life. You can't be afraid of time – easier said than done, obviously, since that is clearly the thing I fear most of all.

You can't be afraid of people, of throwing yourself at them.

Life is, in the long run, only those risks which you did and did not take.

You can't be afraid of nakedness, of diving head first with nothing on into the vast expanse of your existence with a total stranger.

You have to be vulnerable.

Vulnerability is the most delicious kind of bittersweet.

It can be something that gets you hurt, but it can also be something that gets you one step closer to whatever it is you're looking for.

Be vulnerable and

take horrible risks and casual ones

and never

for even one, single second

obsess

over the ticking of the clock.

One day you'll wake up and it won't even surprise you that,

at last,

what you've been searching for is
sleeping on the pillow next to
yours.

About the Author

Rachel Jeffries lives in Lone Tree, Colorado, and regularly travels with her parents to their residence in Scottsdale, Arizona.

Rachel is a 17 year old senior at Valor Christian High School in Highlands Ranch, Colorado. Rachel maintains a heavy AP course load with Duke University as her collegiate goal, and law school to follow. Rachel serves as Editor-in-Chief of *True Blue,* the school newspaper, and loves supporting Valor Theatre productions.

Rachel has studied Taekwondo since her childhood, and is working towards her 4th Degree Black Belt. In the coming months, Rachel will also earn her Gold Award in Girl Scouts of America.

In addition to this book, Rachel has published two young adult novels, *Playing Fairy Godmother* and *Finding My Brother's Princess*.

www.ingramcontent.com/pod-product-compliance
Lightning Source LLC
Chambersburg PA
CBHW061155040426
42445CB00013B/1686